The
Swallow

Published by Raintree Steck-Vaughn Publishers, an imprint of Steck-Vaughn Company.

Acknowledgments
Project Editor: Helene Resky
Design Manager: Joyce Spicer
Consulting Editor: Kim Merlino
Consultant: Michael Chinery
Illustrated by Malcolm Ellis
Designed by Ian Winton and Steve Prosser
Electronic Cover Production: Alan Klemp
Additional Electronic Production: Bo McKinney and Scott Melcer
Photography credits on page 32

Planned and produced by The Creative Publishing Company

Library of Congress Cataloging-in-Publication Data
Crewe, Sabrina
The swallow / Sabrina Crewe.
p.   cm. — (Life cycles)
Includes index.
Summary: Describes the habitat, eating habits, and life cycle of the barn swallow.
ISBN 0-8172-4373-9 (hardcover). — ISBN 0-8172-6236-9 (pbk.)
1. Swallows — Juvenile literature.   2. Barn swallow — Juvenile literature.   3. Swallows — Life cycles — Juvenile literature.   4. Barn swallow — Life cycles — Juvenile literature.
[1. Barn swallow.   2. Swallows.]   I. Title.   II. Series: Crewe, Sabrina. Life cycles.
QL696.P247C74   1997
598.8′13 — dc20   96-4832
                                                   CIP   AC

1 2 3 4 5 6 7 8 9 0 LB 00 99 98 97 96
Printed and bound in the United States of America.

Words explained in the glossary appear in
bold the first time they are used in the text.

The
Swallow

Sabrina Crewe

RSVP

RAINTREE STECK-VAUGHN
P U B L I S H E R S
The Steck-Vaughn Company

Austin, Texas

The swallows are making a nest.

It is spring. The swallows are gathering mud and feathers. They have found a safe place in a barn to make their nest.

The nest is ready.

The swallows have mixed the mud with
grass and animal hair to make the nest strong.
They have lined the nest with feathers. After
eight days, the nest is finished.

The eggs are in the nest.

The female swallow has laid her eggs. Inside the eggs, **embryos** are growing into swallow chicks. They feed on the egg **yolk**.

The swallow sits on the eggs.

The parent swallows take turns sitting on the eggs. This keeps the eggs warm and helps the chicks grow. They grow inside the eggs for two weeks.

The chick hatches from its egg.

Chicks use their beaks to crack open their eggshells. When they come out, swallow chicks have no feathers. They cannot fly or feed themselves.

The chick has grown quickly.

Now the chick is nine days old. Its
eyes are open, and it is much bigger.
The chick looks very different because
it has grown feathers.

The chicks are very hungry!

The parent swallows work hard all day to feed their chicks. They catch insects and bring them back to the nest. The parents push the insects into the chicks' mouths.

The parent birds have other jobs to do.
They keep **predators** away from the chicks.
They also clean and fix the nest.

The fledgling stretches its wings.

The little swallows are two weeks
old. Now they are called **fledglings**.
Soon they will be ready to fly.

The fledglings are out of the nest.

The fledglings are four weeks old. They have learned to fly. The parent swallows still feed the fledglings and look after them. At night, the fledglings go back to their nest.

The swallows have left the nest.

The young swallows are ready to look after themselves. Now they can sleep outside. They may spend the night in the **reeds** near a pond or lake.

The swallow is taking a drink.

Swallows like to live near water. When they are thirsty, swallows drink as they fly just above the water.

The swallow catches an insect.

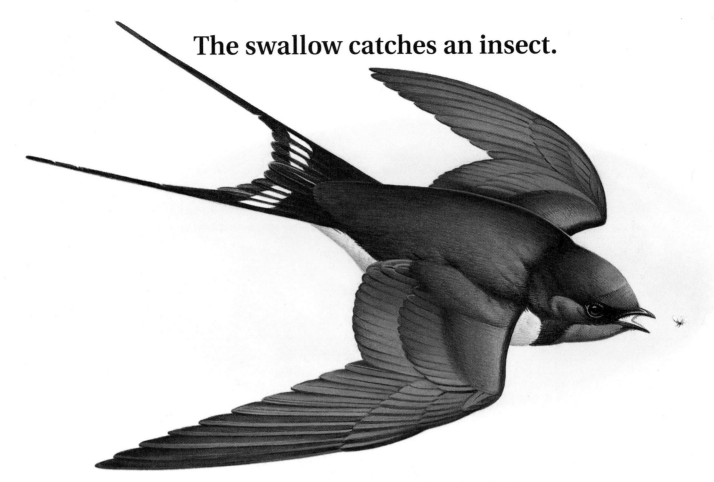

Swallows catch all their food while
they are flying. They move much better
in the air than they do on the ground.
When a swallow sees an insect, it moves
fast to trap the insect in its beak.

In the summer, swallows eat as many insects as they can find. They need to store **energy** and make themselves strong.

The swallow has grown new feathers.

The swallow is six months old. Its old feathers have fallen out. In their place are strong, new feathers. The swallow is getting ready to fly a long way.

The swallows gather together.

It is fall. The days are getting shorter and cooler, and there are not many insects around. The swallows know it is time to leave. They have come together to form a **flock**.

The swallows are migrating.

The flock starts its **migration** to a warmer place. Many young swallows are making the journey for the first time. Their **instinct** tells them which way to go.

The swallows travel thousands of miles.
They travel over deserts and jungles. It
is a long and dangerous journey. Every
night the swallows stop to rest.

The swallows rest in the sun.

After eight weeks, the swallows reach
their winter home. It is very warm, and
there are plenty of insects for them to eat.
The swallows will stay here all winter.

The swallows have returned.

In the spring, the swallows come back to their summer home. They are very tired after their long journey. When the young swallow has rested, it will look for a mate.

The swallows are ready to mate.

In the spring, swallows mate to **fertilize** the female's eggs. Then young swallows make nests with their new mates. Older pairs find their nests from the year before.

Swallows need safe places to make nests.

Swallows help people by eating mosquitoes and other harmful insects. Fewer insect pests means less damage to plants. People can help swallows by **protecting** their nests and leaving the swallows alone to raise their young.

Parts of a Swallow

Swallows are birds. Birds are covered in feathers. They have two wings, and nearly all of them can fly. Birds give birth to their young by laying eggs.

Wings
Long and pointed

Forked tail
Used for steering and braking

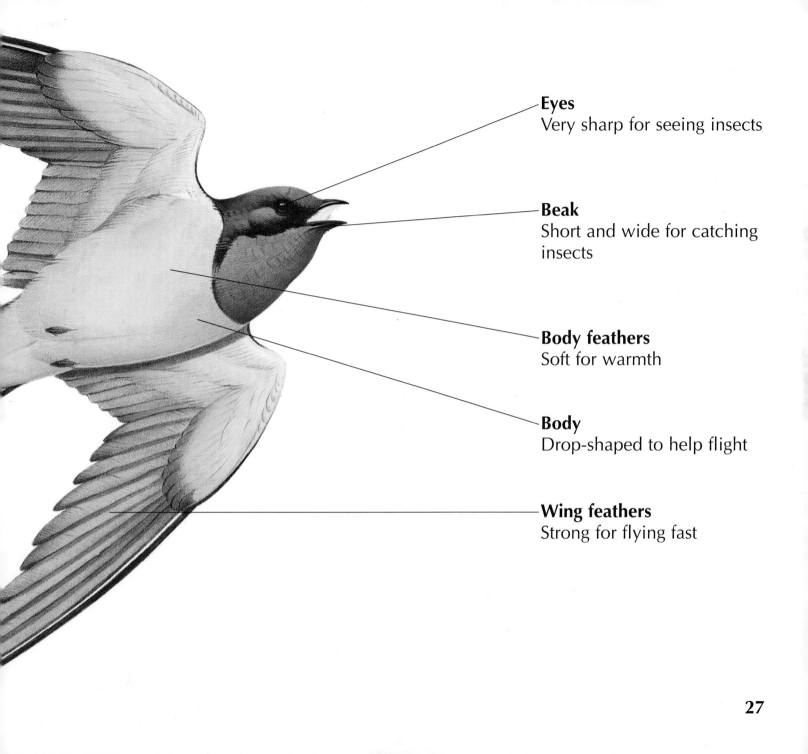

Eyes
Very sharp for seeing insects

Beak
Short and wide for catching insects

Body feathers
Soft for warmth

Body
Drop-shaped to help flight

Wing feathers
Strong for flying fast

Other Birds

The swallow in this book is a barn swallow. Here are some other swallows and different kinds of birds. Two of these birds are not able to fly. The penguin's wings are in the form of flippers for swimming, and the ostrich is too heavy to fly.

Ruby-throated hummingbird

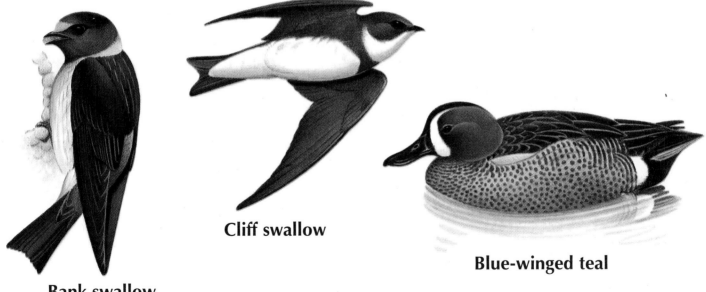

Cliff swallow

Bank swallow

Blue-winged teal

Great horned owl

Golden eagle

Rockhopper penguin

Green-cheeked
Amazon parrot

Ostrich

Where the Barn Swallow Lives

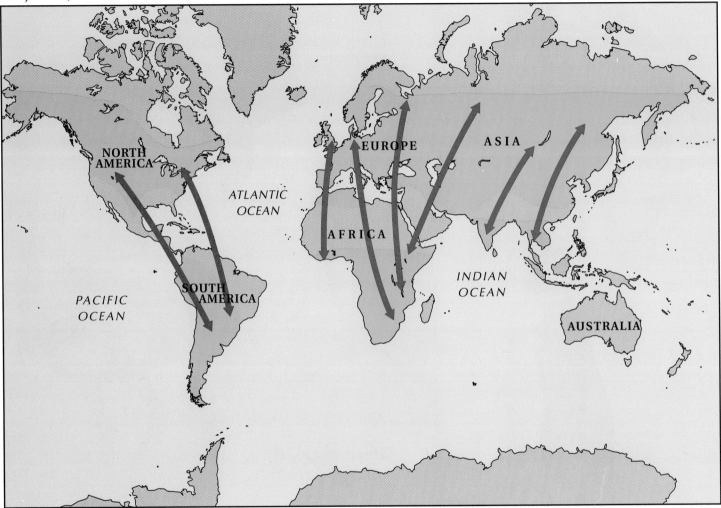

Areas where the barn swallow lives

Migratory routes of the barn swallow

Glossary

Embryo An animal in the first growing stages before it is born

Energy The power to do things

Fertilize To make a female's eggs able to produce babies

Fledgling A young bird that is learning or has just learned to fly

Flock A large group of birds

Instinct A way of behaving with which an animal is born

Migration The move from one place to another when the seasons change

Predator An animal that hunts and kills other animals for food

Protect To keep safe

Reeds Tall, thin grass

Yolk The yellow part of an egg, which provides food to the embryo

Index